A COLLECTION

JAPANESE DESIGN

A COLLECTION

JAPANESE DESIGN

KENNETH STRAITON

WEATHERHILL
NEW YORK / TOKYO

First edition, 1999
Published by Weatherhill, Inc., of
New York and Tokyo. Protected by copyright under the terms of the International
Copyright Union; all rights reserved.
Except for fair use in book reviews, no part
of this book may be reproduced for any
reason by any means, including any
method of photographic reproduction,
without permission of the Weatherhill, Inc.
Printed in Hong Kong.

05 04 03 02 01 00 6 5 4 3 2 1

Library of Congress
Cataloging-in Publication Data
Straiton, Kenneth.
Japanese design : a collection /
photographs by Kenneth Straiton. --
      p.   cm.
ISBN 0–8348–0455–7
1. Design--Japan Pictorial works. I. Title.
NK1484.A1S77   1999
745.4'4952--dc21   99–39263
CIP

Contents

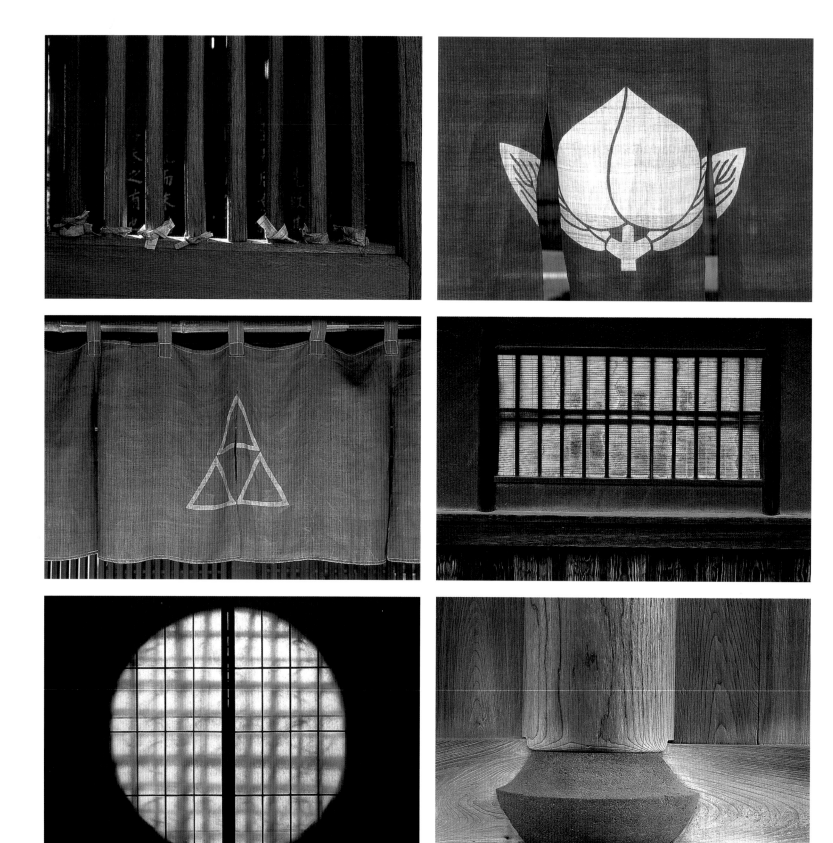

Foreword

Stroll down any street in Japan—a grand commercial avenue like modern Tokyo's Ginza or a back lane in a rural village—and one's vision is filled with signs, symbols, patterns, and designs. To the newcomer, unaccustomed to the surrounding visual language, Japan is an assault on the eye, a cacophony of imagery. The sheer density of the tapestry of images seems impossible to penetrate, and the accumulation of unfamiliar signs and illegible signifiers is bewildering and overwhelming. Unable to read, to sort, to comprehend, the viewer feels besieged by a vast army of visual messages, overpowered by the chaotic intensity of the attack. Overpowered, yet intrigued. The beauty of the patterns is undeniably seductive, the juxtaposition of colors irresistibly alluring.

In time, fragments of meaning begin to emerge from the visual chaos. One slowly comes to comprehend, or rather to apprehend, an order, and one's eyes seek out details, small messages that give comfort. One begins to isolate individual images, ponder them, and to assign to them meaning. In similar fashion, the lens of Kenneth Straiton's camera has for nearly twenty years sought out messages and patterns from the rich array of imagery presented by Japanese modern and traditional life. As Straiton has looked deeper and deeper into Japan, he has found solace in the details. And more than solace: wisdom and poetry. Sorting, culling, and editing the many thousands of impressions captured by his camera over two decades, he has brought an order, a pattern and disci-

pline, to the myriad flashes of intuitive understanding captured through the shutter. Here, Kenneth Straiton presents his Japan. It is a personal view, uniquely his, but it also has a universality that will be recognized by any visitor to that country.

The French poet, philosopher, and aesthetician Roland Barthes wrestled with Japan in similar fashion, and came away calling it the Empire of Signs. Challenged by his encounters with Japan, and clearly invigorated by his travels there, he attempted to integrate his many impressions and struggled to give them meaning in words. Barthes's meditations on Japan resulted in what may be the finest expression of that elusive science known as semiotics, but they somehow lack the precision of the images in these pages. His objective and Kenneth Straiton's may have been much the same: to capture and to comprehend the essence of a seductive culture. But here the photographer has the advantage over the essayist, for Japan gives up its meanings more readily through a language that is visual rather than verbal. The "reader" of this book of images will form his own interpretations and come to his own conclusions: though Straiton's pictures hint at meanings and suggest associations, they do not analyze or explain.

Contemporary Japan is a vigorous society, full of creative energy and artistic and intellectual ferment, and one might think that its restless dynamism could be captured only by a motion-picture camera. However the still photographs of this book belie this assumption through their surprising display of movement and vigor. Water trickles and waves crash and roar, even if they do so here in a two-dimensional rendering on fabric or paper, or in the abstraction of stone and sand in a Japanese garden. Festival crowds surge and dance, even though we see and hear them only through images of rows of lanterns, myriad masks, and heaps of Daruma dolls. Traffic flows ceaselessly through alleys and avenues, and we feel the rhythm through the architectural patterns lining the streets. The expressive energy of the poet or master calligrapher is still felt in the brushed writing left behind on paper.

Immediately evident as well in these pages is that all imagery in Japan derives from Nature. The Japanese spiritual relationship with the natural world is close, intimate, and inescapable. So often has this simple truth been repeated by writers about Japan, both native and foreign, that it is now a cliché, but that does not render it any less true. Some regard the Japanese affinity for natural imagery in everyday life and in every mode of artistic expression a manifestation of animism, others explain it as Shinto-inspired, and still others label it primitivist or innocent or unsophisticated. But regardless of its name or cause, it is clearly there. And although some cultural historians claim that such affinity for Nature is a "premodern" instinct, destined to vanish with industrialization and modernization, it seems to endure in Japan. It is as recognizable in the *manga* animations of late twentieth-century Japanese popular culture as it was a millennium ago in the poetry of the *Man'yoshu* or the *Kokinshu*.

Kenneth Straiton's work clearly shows that images of the natural world and not the abstractions of the intellect have motivated Japanese artists, designers, architects, and decorators. While natural objects may be rendered abstractly through simplification or through transformation into ideograms or geometrical designs, their source imagery remains clear. Consider, for example, the many versions of the pattern of flowing water. Japan is an island nation, surrounded by oceans, where rain falls nearly a third of every year, and where the land is everywhere watered by brooks, streams, waterfalls, and rivers. The very staff of life, rice, is grown in watery paddies. Should it be any surprise that water possess such powerful symbolism there? Artistic expressions of rain, waves, and rivers are everywhere: in paintings and garden design, of course, but also in architectural elements such as roof tiles, in textile designs, in handcrafted paper and lacquerware, in the arrangement of a plate of *sashimi* or a serving of cold noodles, or in the wrapping of condiments and candies. The same can be said of design patterns derived from flowers and grasses, from the forms of birds and fish, or from the natural grain of wood. Nature and its infinite forms and patterns are never far from the mind of the designer or artist in Japan.

It has been said that the form of Japanese writing is the link between the physical manifestations of the natural world and the expressive renderings and abstractions of the Japanese artist or craftsman. This form is not uniquely Japanese, of course. The ideograms of Japanese writing were inherited from China, where concrete objects of the natural world were first expressed in easily recognizable "picture words." In time, abstract concepts also came to be rendered in combinations of picture-based ideograms. In premodern China and Japan, all writing was done with a brush dipped in black ink on absorbent handmade paper. Learning to write ideograms instilled principles of balance and propor-

tion. Characters are written in a prescribed stroke order that incorporates discipline and an almost musical sense of rhythm and movement. The essence of the ideogram-based writing system is this fusion of the choreography of the arm and hand with the intellectual discipline of absorbing meaning. It should come as no surprise that anyone learning to write this way should simultaneously develop an instinct and appreciation for good design and proportion in all things. This is not to say that all Chinese or Japanese are necessarily great artists or designers, but simply that the fundamental tools of artistic expression were, throughout history, instilled through the ordinary processes of acquiring literacy. Today, as the computer and word processor supplant the ink stick and the writing brush, the consequences for artistic expressiveness are hard to predict. The advance indicators, however, are not encouraging.

Kenneth Straiton's images offer us a vision of beauty. There are colors and designs that will strike the eye forcefully and leave an enduring impact. There appears a lovely harmony of literal imagery and abstraction, of form and function, of pattern and significance that the sensitive viewer will find deeply satisfying. But there is even more. The photographs are glimpses that beckon one to look further and to ponder more deeply. Through these pictures one can discover a culture that is rich, varied, and seamlessly integrated; a worldview that remains close to Nature and values simplicity over complexity; one that cherishes natural materials and natural forms, allowing the genius of the artist or the hand of the craftsman to enrich them through pattern and design, giving them universal validity and enduring value. These pictures present a world in which present time is anchored firmly in the traditions of the past, and, nurtured by those traditions, finds the strength to discover the future.

—Peter Grilli

P r e f a c e

Some people say that photographers are collectors by nature. Surely something of that is reflected in this collection of images, but more important is their documentation of creations that I find profoundly moving. The subjects show a certain genius, there is no other word for it.

This book began unconsciously, during my first trip to Japan, in 1982.

At the time I was a photographer and artist, and although I had yet to begin a commercial career, I had always been interested in design. I had studied art history and architecture, traveled to Europe a number of times, and had worked on furniture and houses, including some of my own designs. While I had found in Europe a design legacy that was largely decorative, and to some extent, extraneous, in Japan I recognized in what I saw an aesthetic that was closer to the heart of what I was trying to work with myself.

Coming from the Western tradition, where design is often decoration, relying on symmetry and elaboration, it was a revelation to see the subtlety and strength of Japanese designs. They worked within a traditional Asian framework, but seemed to contain all the essentials of the Western Modernist style. I started to collect images of striking and even simple but quintessential designs. This sensitized me to the host of details everywhere around me, even in the midst of an increasingly modern, reconstructed Tokyo. There is really nothing much like it in the environment of my native Canada, or North America,

except perhaps in the decorative elements of buildings from the Art Deco period, and earlier. But in Japan the difference is that these are not just decoration, but symbols and allusions to be read.

There is something delightful, like secret messages, about these silent images residing all around. It is a constant reminder of the past, and of the depth of the culture. Perhaps contemporary Japanese are beginning to lose the ability to interpret these messages from their communal subconscious.

In time, when I could afford it, I began to buy old items with the intent to photograph them (clever rationalist that I am), and this led me to investigate the history and meaning of different designs. However, it is not my intent here to *explain* Japanese design. When trying to define what precisely characterizes it, the attempt inevitably founders on the exceptions. It is not one thing, one style, or set of principles, yet there is undeniably a common underlying quality that sets it apart. That surprising asymmetrical slash of color, perhaps inspired by Zen philosophy, may be a part of a tradition handed down from China, but it has evolved far and in a quintessentially Japanese way. The splash of ink, or the drip of a glaze, the rocks in a garden, are part of a connoisseurship of the phenomenal and transitory. At the same time, this drama, or these uncontrolled organic elements, exist within, and are counterpointed by a framework of rigid and repeated elements that provide a formal structure.

In architecture, at least, it can be argued that this format has evolved from the materials at hand, and certainly the Japanese honor the material in a way that no other culture does. There are aspects that are at once very humble and associated with poverty, while presenting a refinement that is so sophisticated that it denies the obvious and rich. Finally, there is a spirituality that threads its way through it all, connecting it to nature and mortality. In a land where fires and earthquakes pose a constant threat, the fragile elements of the Japanese house, light wooden components framing *tatami* floors and *shoji* paper windows, reinforced perceptions of the transitory nature of things, contributed to a general lightness of effect, and encouraged inventiveness.

It is hard to imagine life in a world where even the materials used to make your clothes or house are regulated by the government, but this was the case under the regime of the Tokugawa shoguns. If one could afford it then, the workmanship and design of an item took on great importance, even when the materials were common. This reality joins with another stream of values from Zen Buddhism, which stress simplicity and honesty, invoking the appreciation of things for their intrinsic value.

There is also a high value placed on the effects of the accumulation of age and the accidental. This is referred to as *sabi*. The appreciation of the uncontrolled extends to new things made with processes that are not entirely predictable, especially in pottery. The design is really in the interaction of materials and the process as mediated by the artist, but, there are also design endeavors in which absolute control is obviously the objective.

There are different styles of decoration, but ultimately almost all traditional decorative design draws on the same constellation of images and symbols. It is the immense variety and ingenuity of use that proves so satisfying, like variations on a musical theme. In Japan's long and insular history, there is almost nothing which has not come to carry some significance. Nearly every motif has meaning beyond its literal reading, with links to literature, poetry, myth, ritual, and the turning of the seasons.

A flower, for example, when used as a decorative element, always carries the allusion to its season, to the point where it really *means* the season, as well as carrying other associations. Items decorated with seasonal references, then, are to be used in season, or just in advance of the season alluded to.

Perhaps this metaphorical reading of references is related to the use of *kanji* (Chinese characters), which also may engender an appreciation of gesture. There is also a tendency to work designs into a flattened plane, rendering them abstracted from reality and deep spatial representations. This dissociation from a strict representation of three-dimensional reality frees the artist to place things on a surface in a much more intuitive fashion. I love the remarkable way that an abstracted scene is overlaid with other elements (often writing) that operate in another plane. The effect is of viewing the design through one or more screens.

Finally, the strength of Japanese design makes it unnecessary to be intimate with all of the historical references to be able to respond to the force or the delicacy of its various manifestations. It seems, rather, that the design goes right to the root of some more primitive shared human understanding.

Nagare

Water and images of water are everywhere in Japan, an island nation blessed with abundant rainfall; water courses through mountain valleys, flows over towering waterfalls, and winds through broad riverbeds to the surrounding seas. Flowing water is a symbol of movement, dynamism, and change. Its only constant quality is its mutability; no rivulet is the same from moment to moment. The ebb and flow of water is a manifestation of the transformative power of nature, as seen in the changing seasons, shifting fortunes, and the rushing journey from birth to death.

Flowing

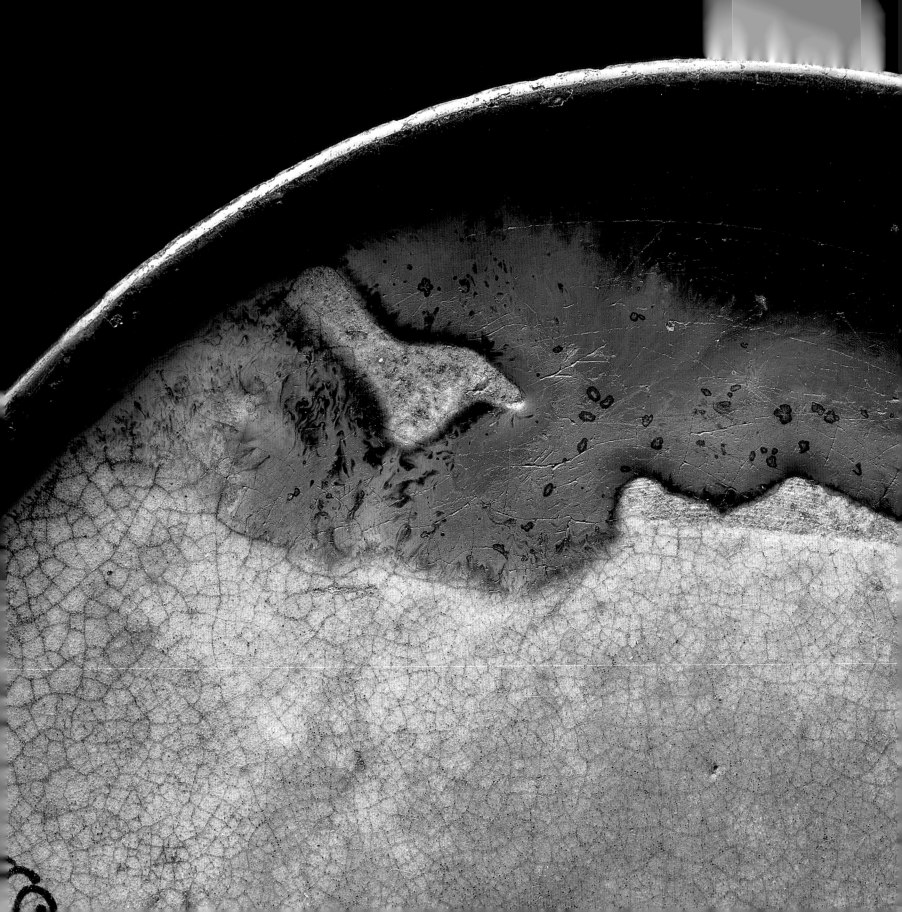

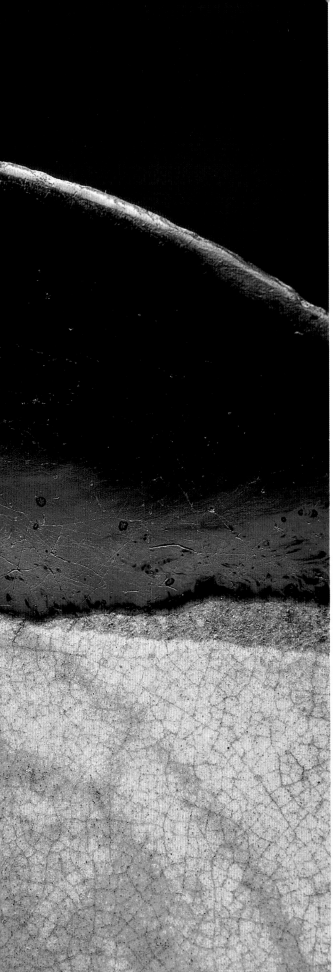

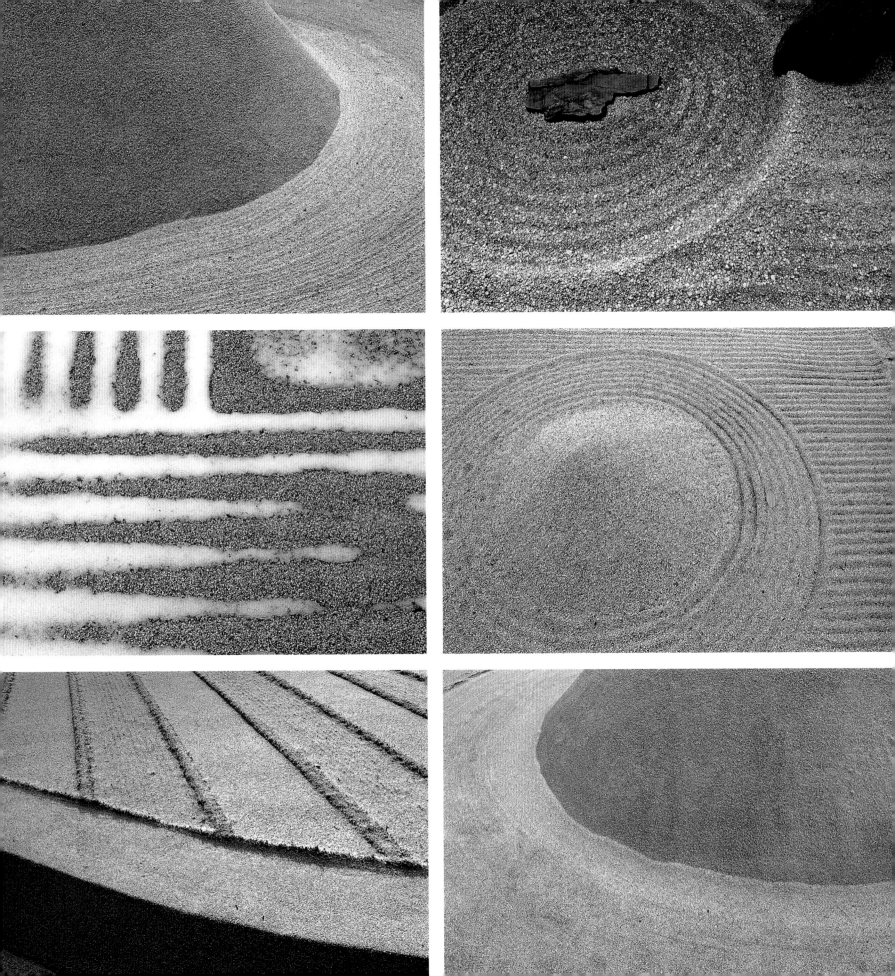

Maru

Extending a point into a line begins a journey that ends only when the line comes "full circle" to return to its starting point. The circle thus symbolizes completion, even perfection. A circle is harmonious and tranquil, yet at the same time it represents the cycle that is life. Spinning unceasingly like the potter's wheel, it creates new forms, enclosing and embracing all of nature's activity—*yin* and *yang,* rise and fall, increase and decrease—within its perfect arc. Finally, the circle is an opening, a window on the whole of being that it also represents, the eye that sees itself.

Circle

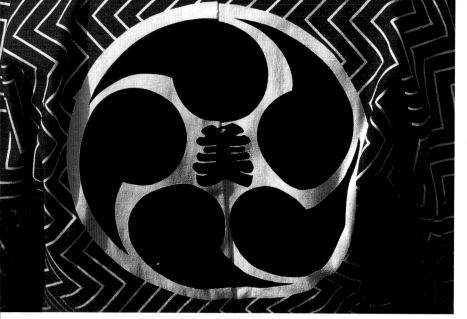

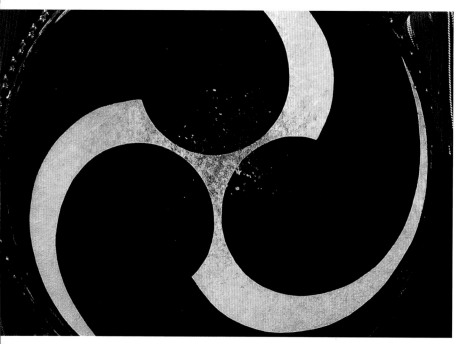

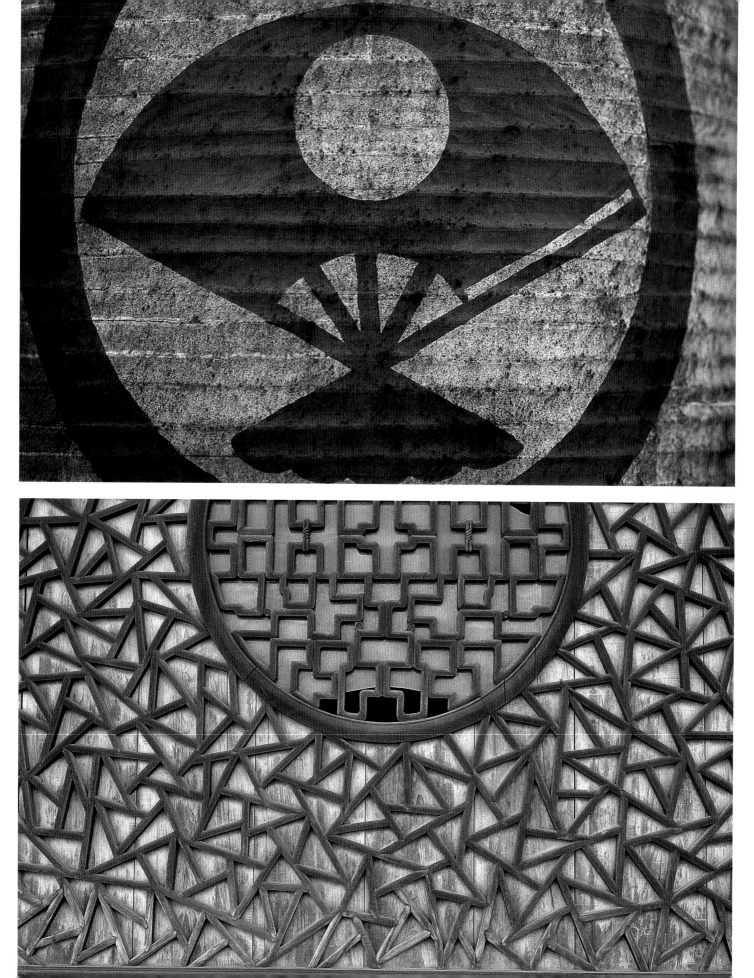

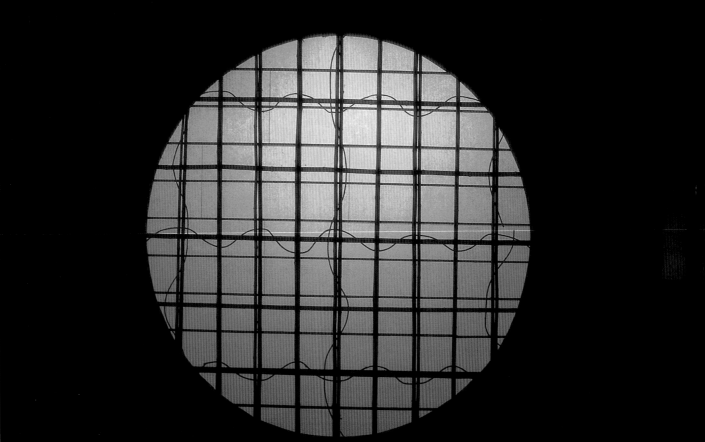

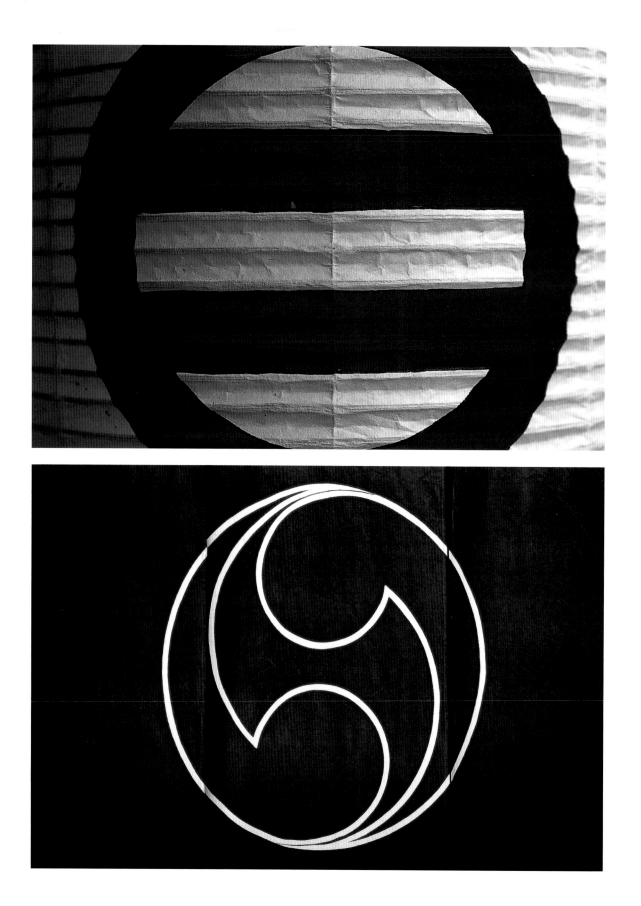

K a t a d o r u

All cultures create signs, but none are as visually expressive as those of the complex Japanese writing system, which incorporates both Chinese characters *(kanji)* and native syllabaries. A *kanji* may be a picture of a thing, or a diagram, or a graphic distillation of its essential form or spirit. Perhaps because of this close link between reality and representation, calligraphy has traditionally been accorded the highest respect in East Asia, even thought capable of revealing one's character. From an early age the Japanese learn to navigate this universe of signs, and use it masterfully to communicate information, evoke moods, and create pure visual beauty.

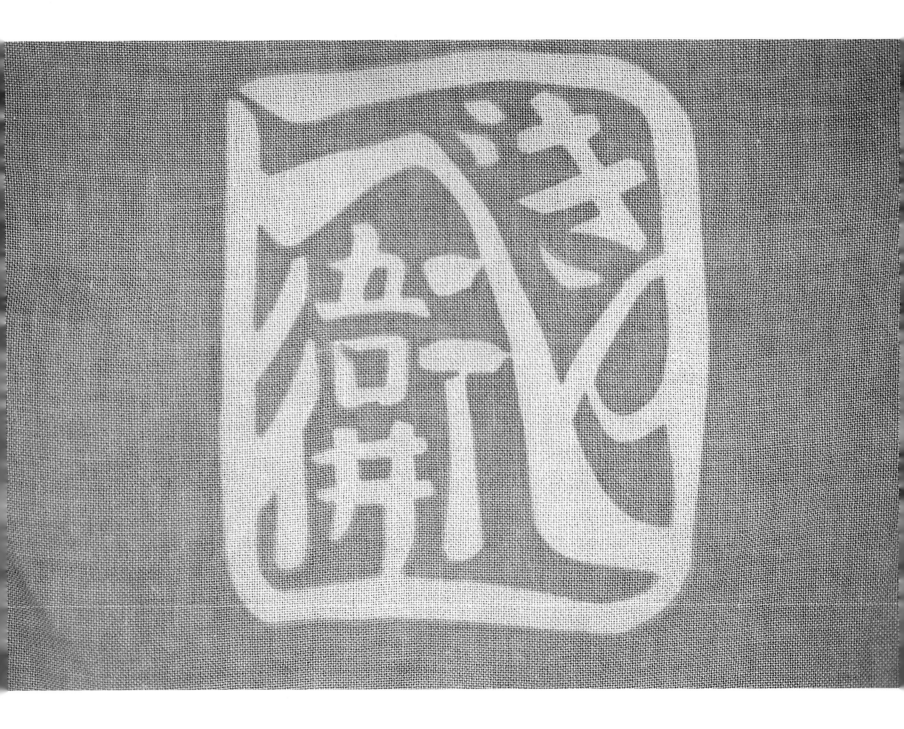

報賽三首歌

民部卿藤原為村

いくちをもしきつ御社のしめ
月きよきめ松乃ふゝゝ

いくちあまよ雪を挿み霜
小野の杜組あかまめくゝゝ
ゝとの梅年ふるゝゝ玉のゝ
をくしきたの杜よ喬流

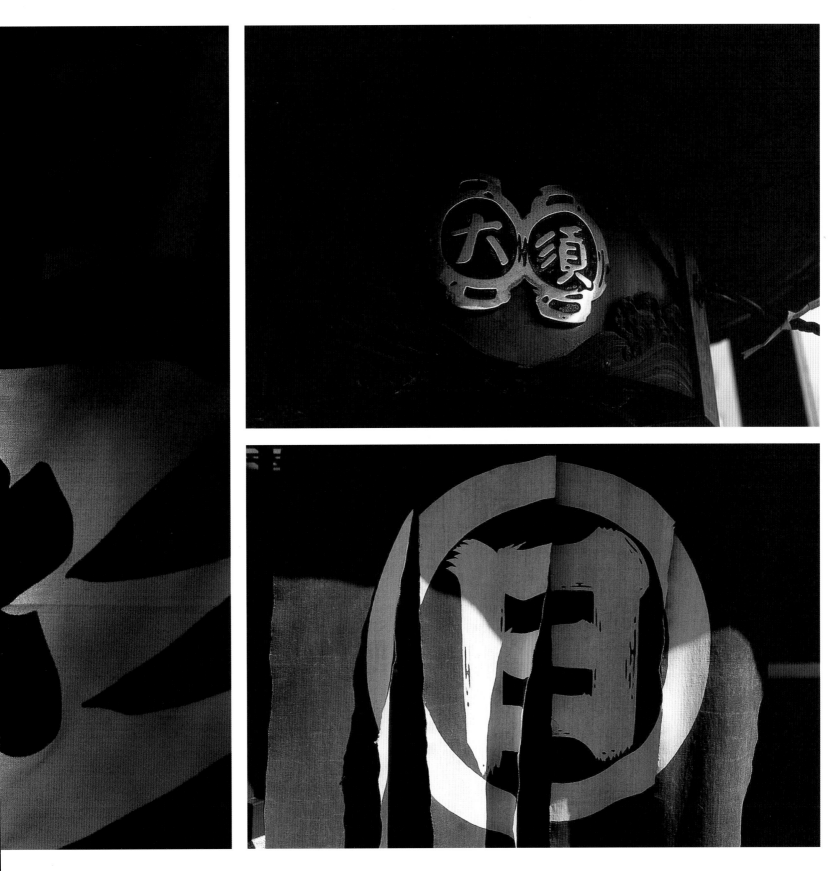

It sometimes seems that nearly anything in Japan can possess sanctity: rocks and trees, waterfalls and streams, animals and plants, and of course the gods, Buddhas, and fabulous creatures such as the ubiquitous dragon, phoenix, and lion-dog. The sacred is announced with braided ropes and twisted paper, with vermilion *torii* gateways, and hulking guardian warriors, while from screens, doors, transoms, rooftops, or clumps of grass by the roadside, painted and carved figures smile or grimace, welcoming worshipers and frightening off malevolent spirits.

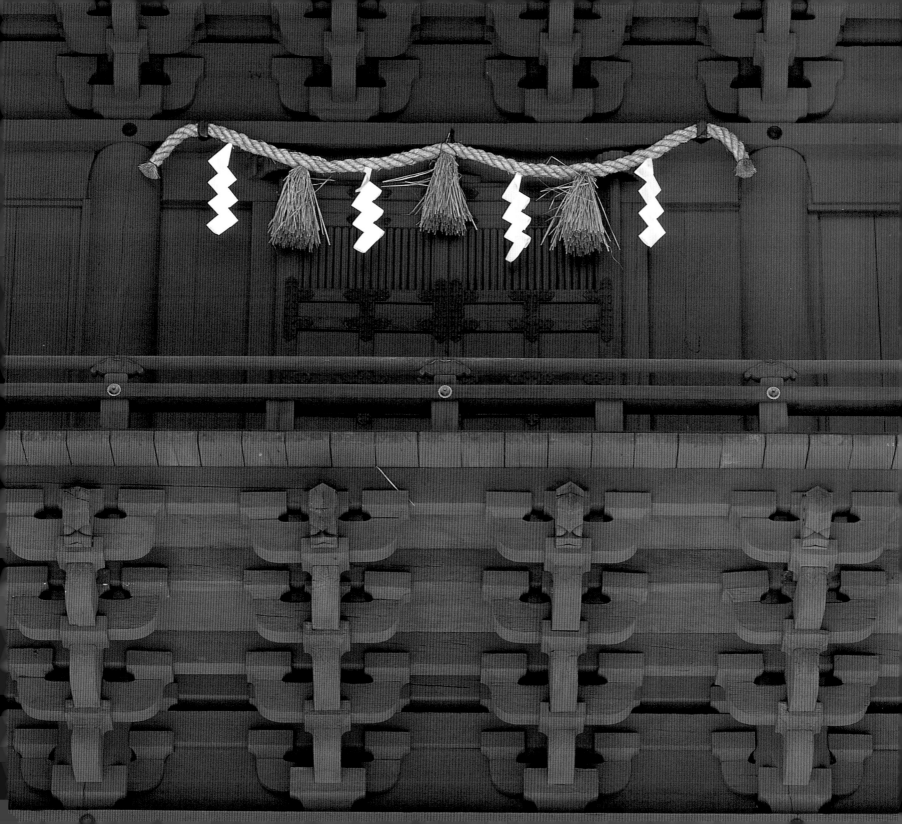

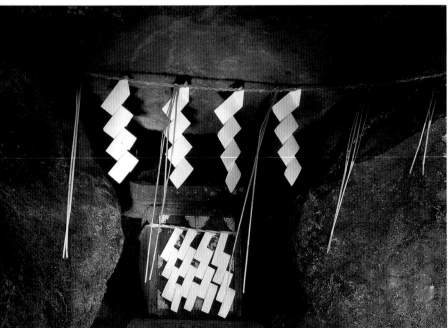

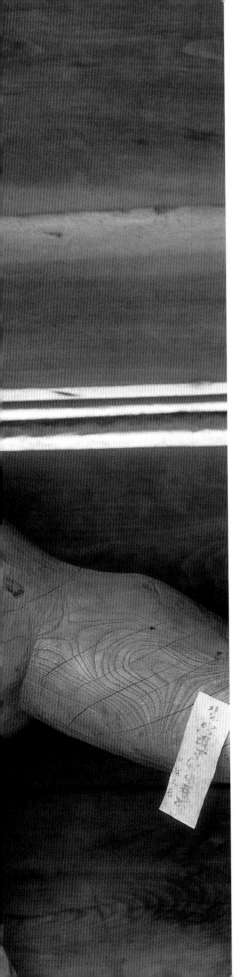

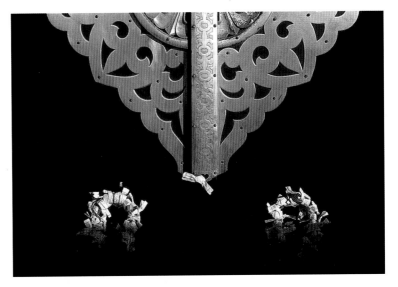

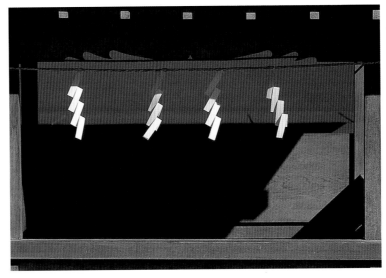

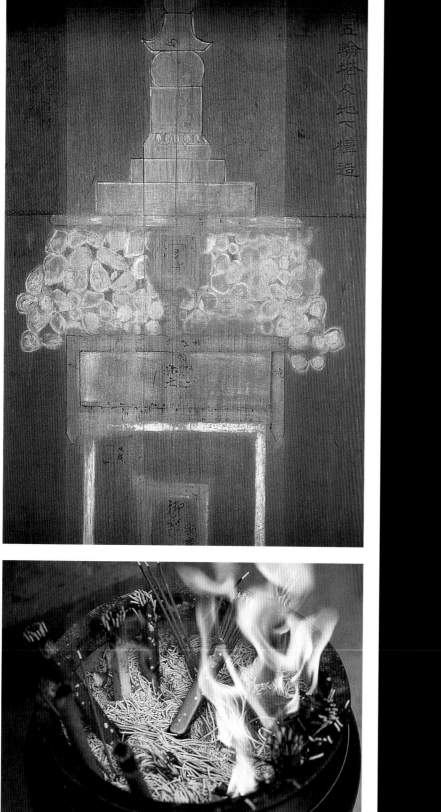

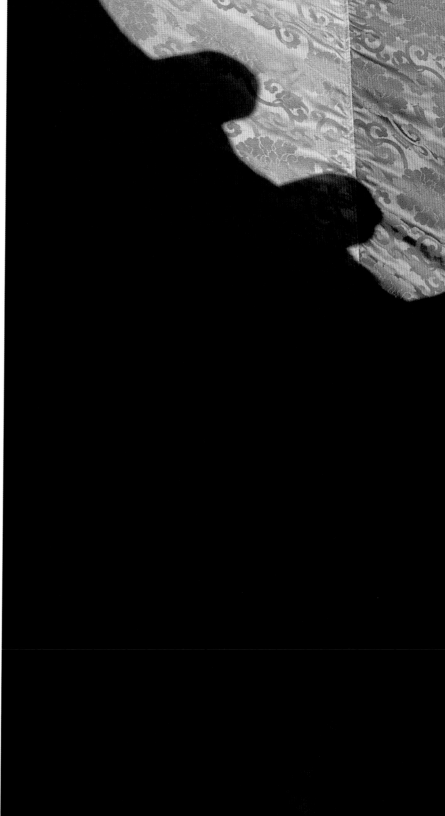

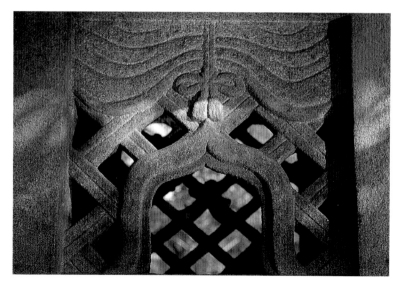

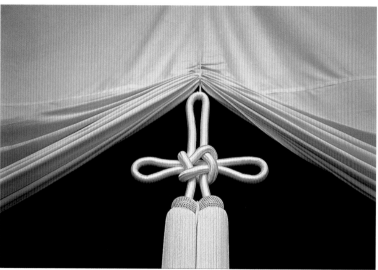

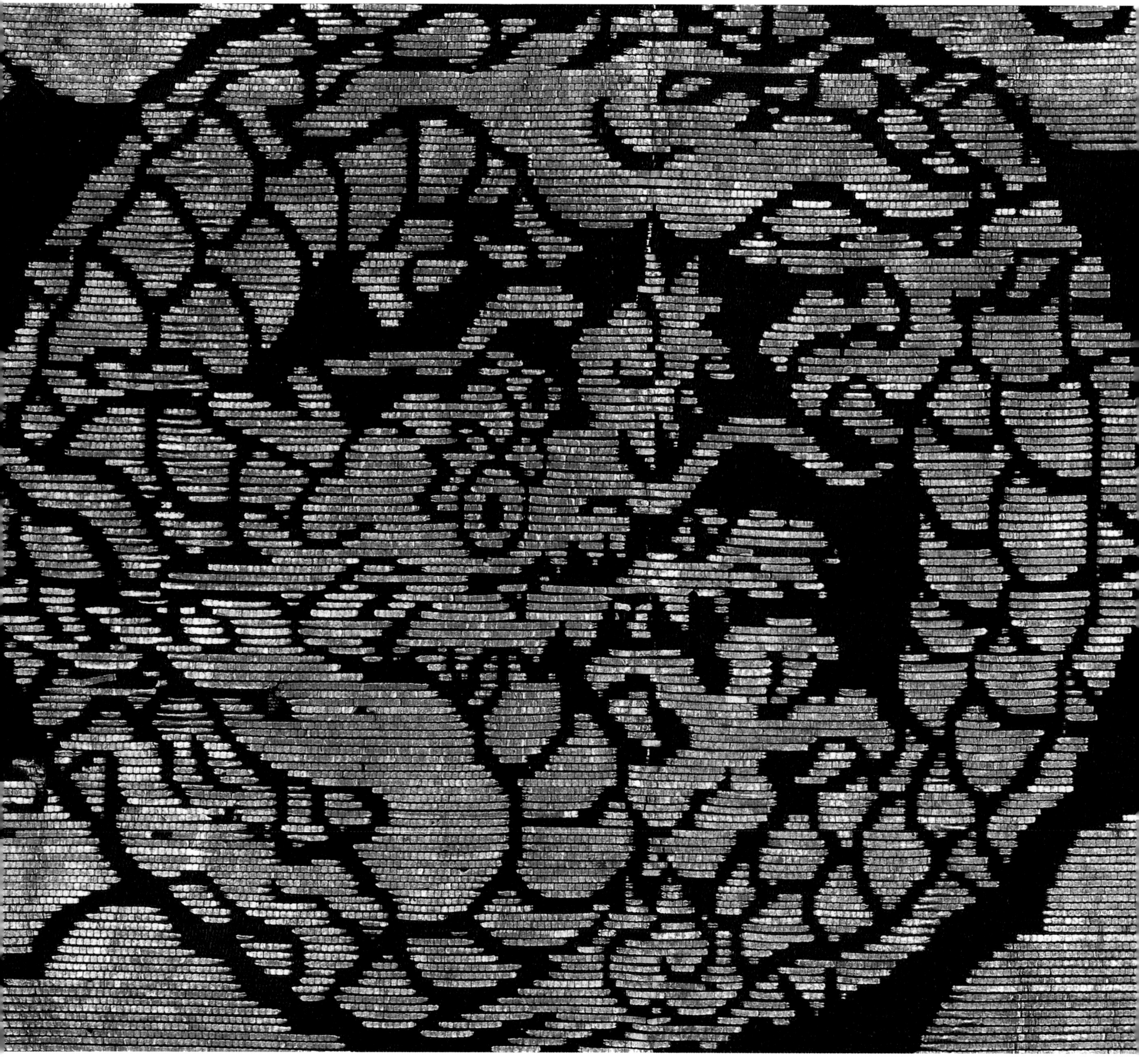

Sei

Nature is the source of all art and design in Japan, the muse of all Japanese artists and designers. The materials of art and architecture are rendered in forms that evoke their natural origins, and artifacts are decorated with images drawn, almost without exception, from the natural world. Over the centuries this process has produced a rich vocabulary of visual imagery in which pine, bamboo, and plum, cherry blossom and iris, carp and crane, all speak eloquently to the viewer, communicating friendship, transience, vigor, fidelity, and a host of other very human emotions and ideas.

Nature

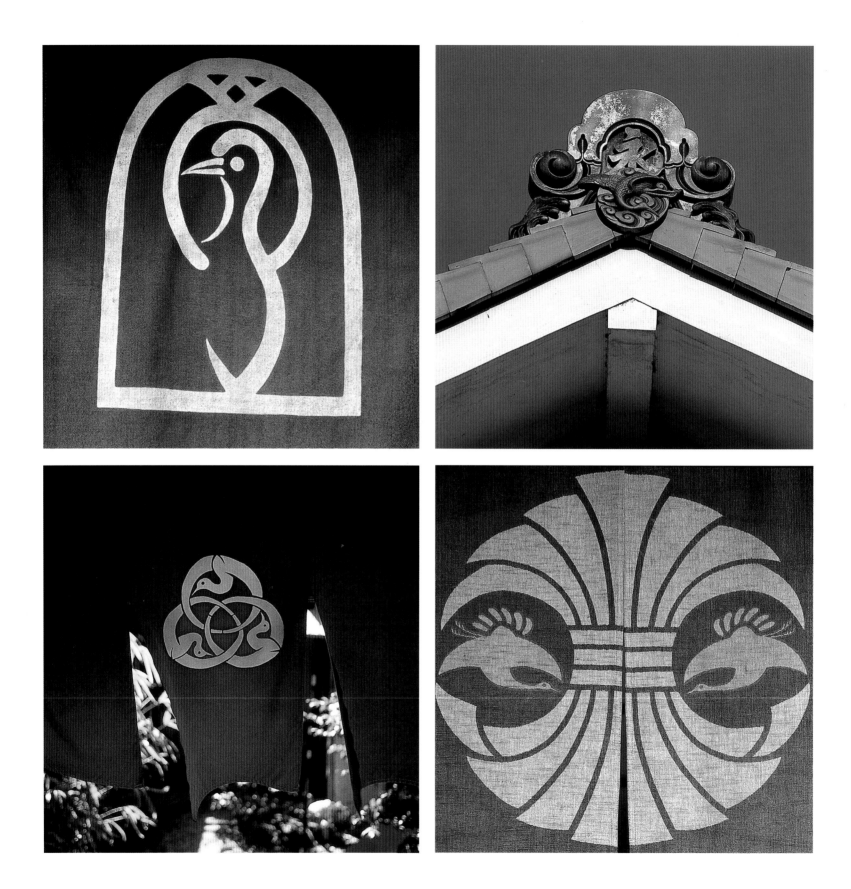

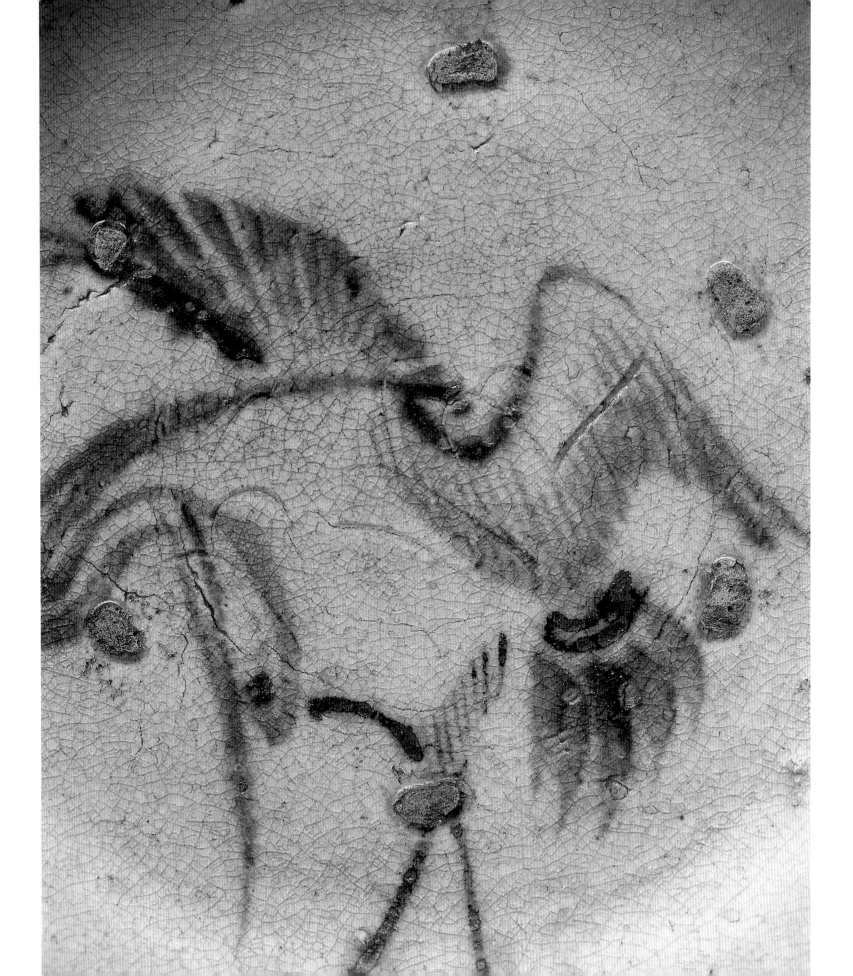

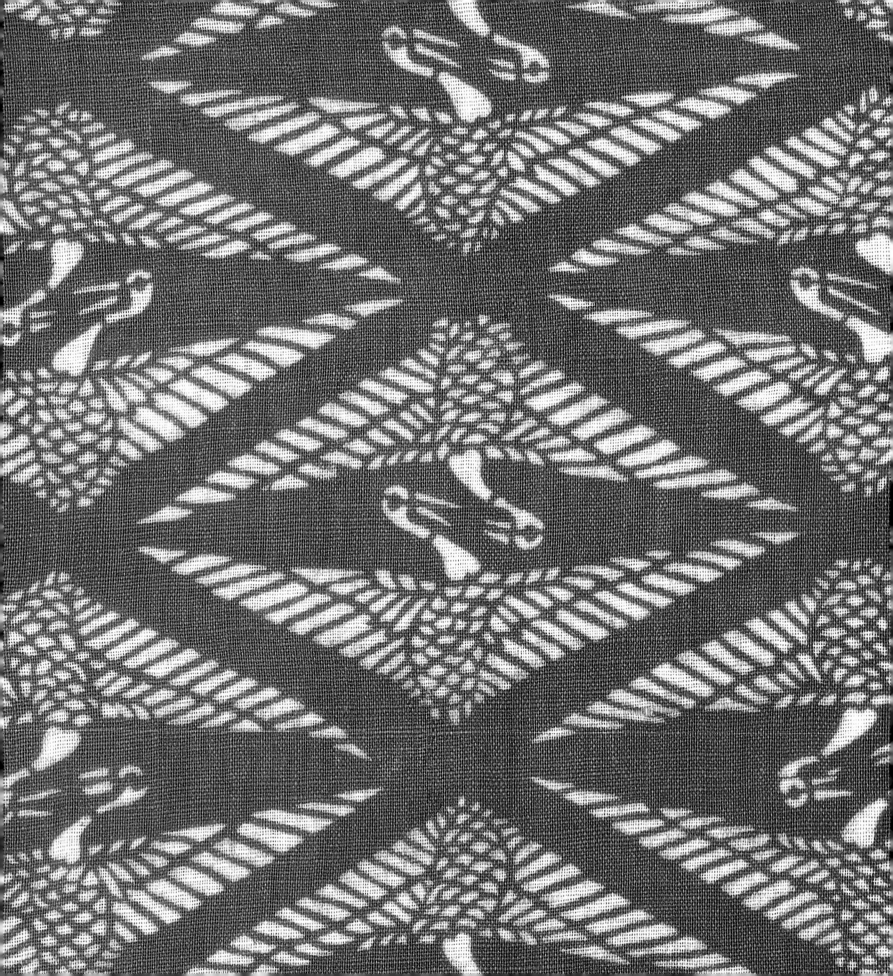

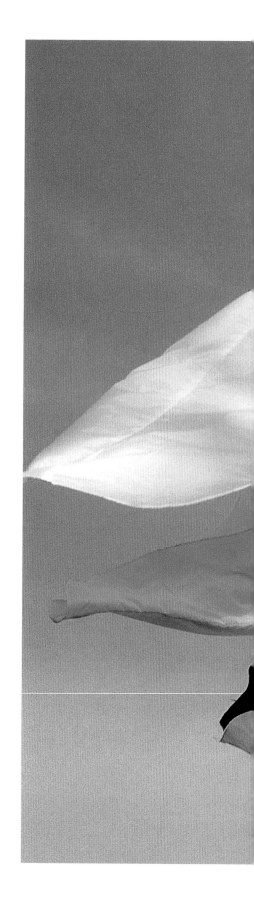

116

Kata

The Japanese have excelled in the ordering of space and visual and architectural elements. Repetition of line and form create serenity and harmony inside and outside the home. Pattern is at work everywhere: the weave of *tatami* floor mats; the strictly proportioned elements of interior space; regular roof lines and the grid of clay roof tiles; exterior walls with strong, repeating horizontal and vertical members; and latticework fences enclosing gardens. These patterns are softened and made more visually engaging by the use of natural materials in their natural forms, thus linking intimately the patterns of human life to those of nature, reminding the individual of his place in the universal order of things.

Pattern

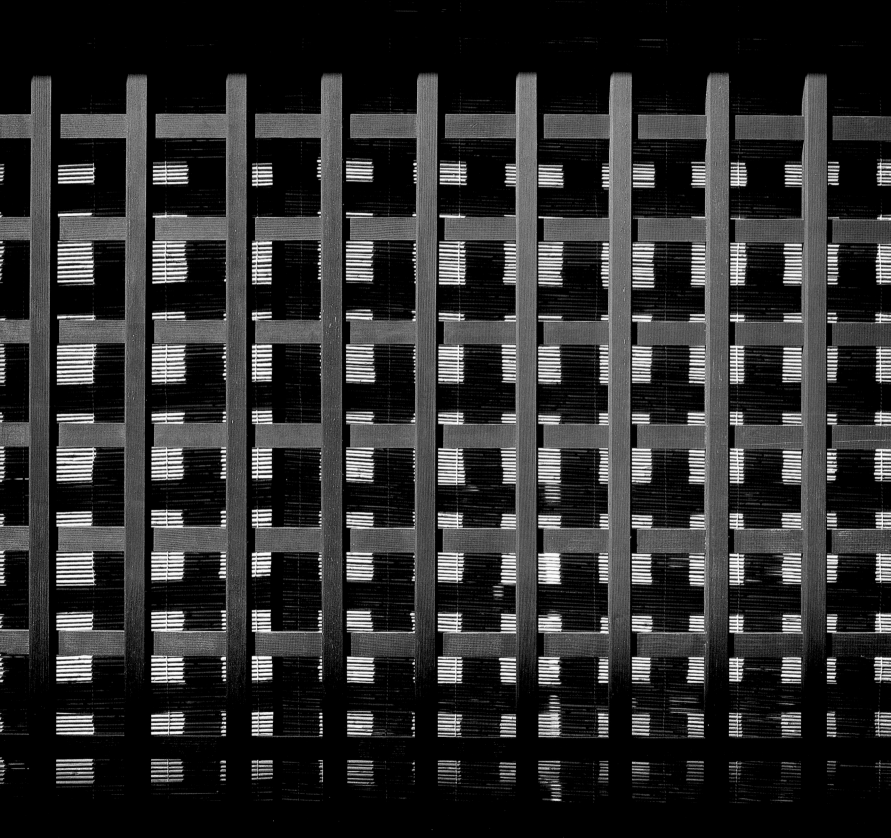

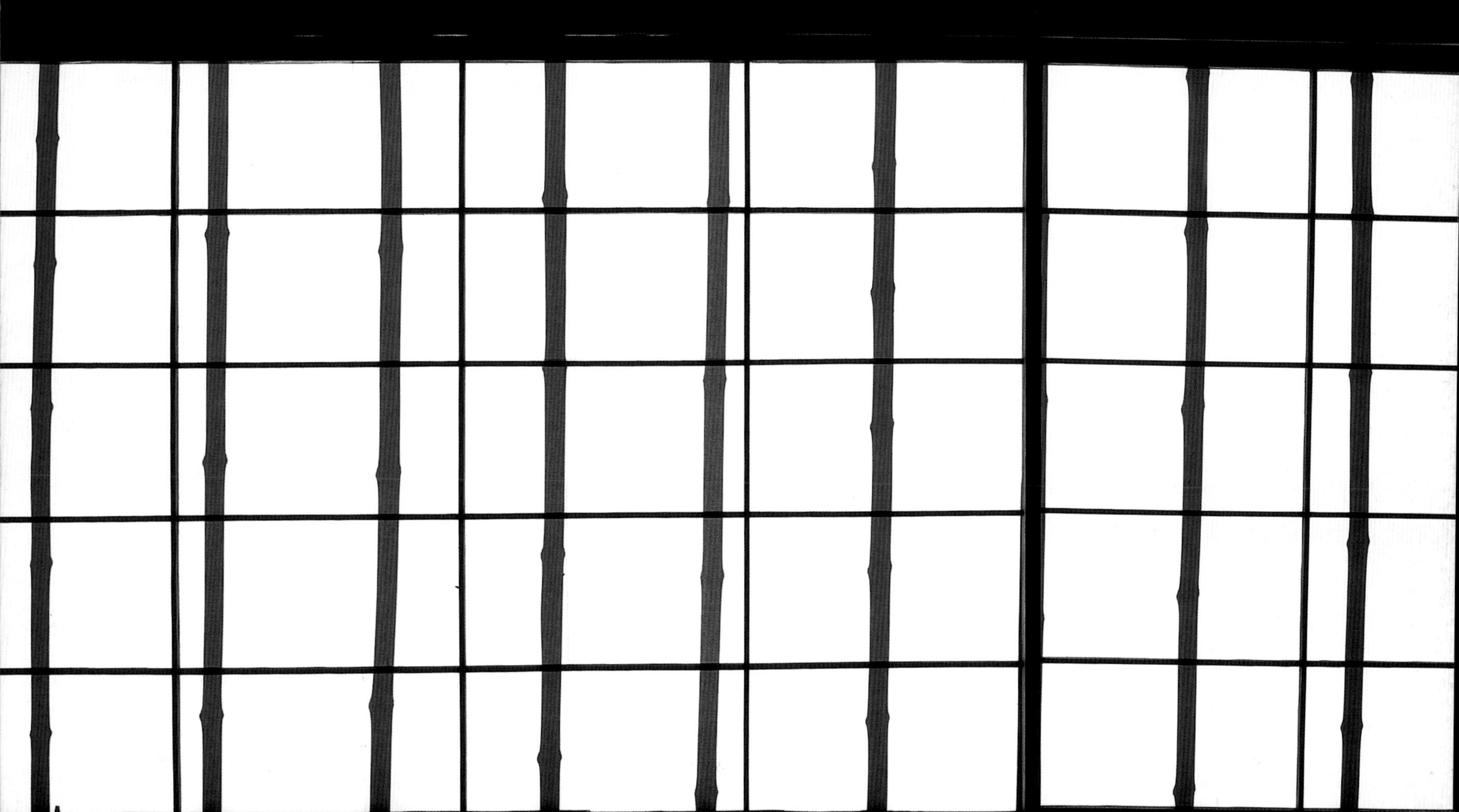

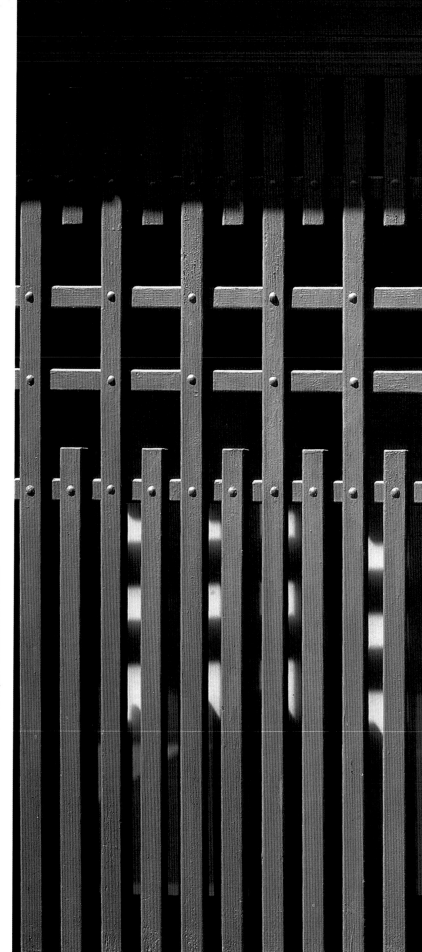

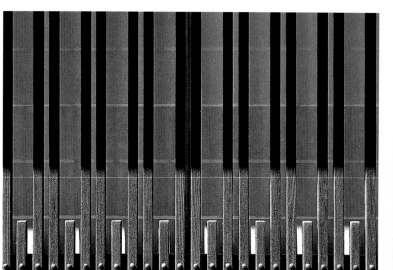

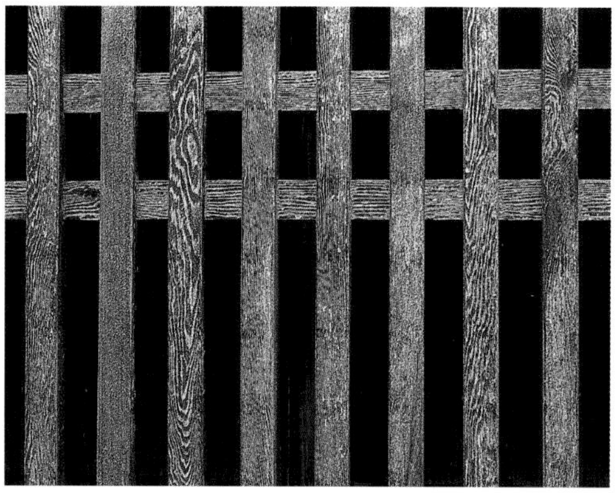
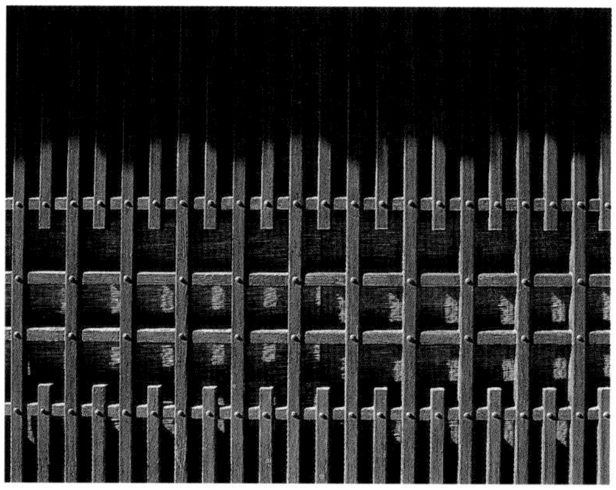

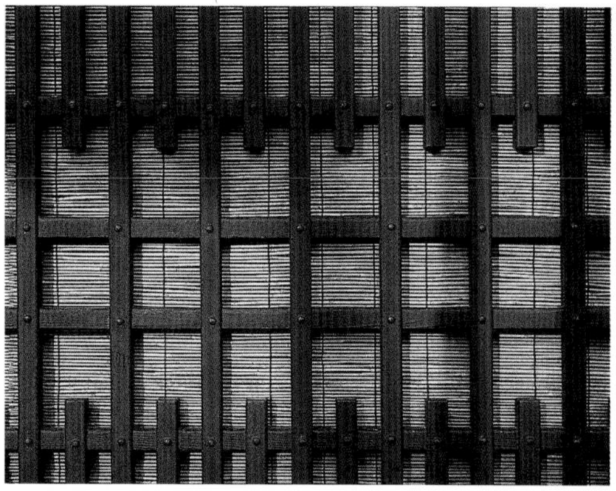
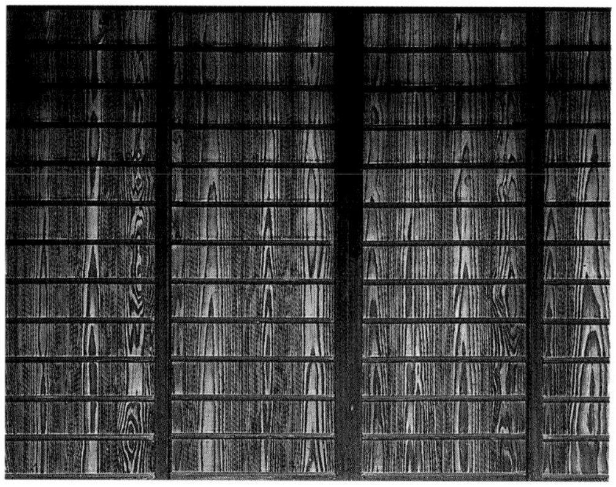
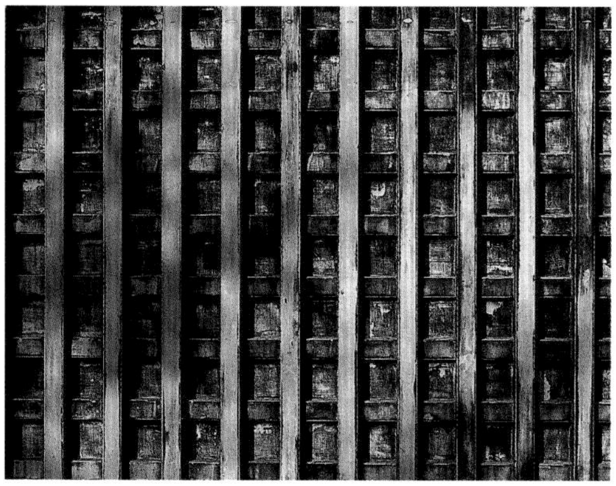
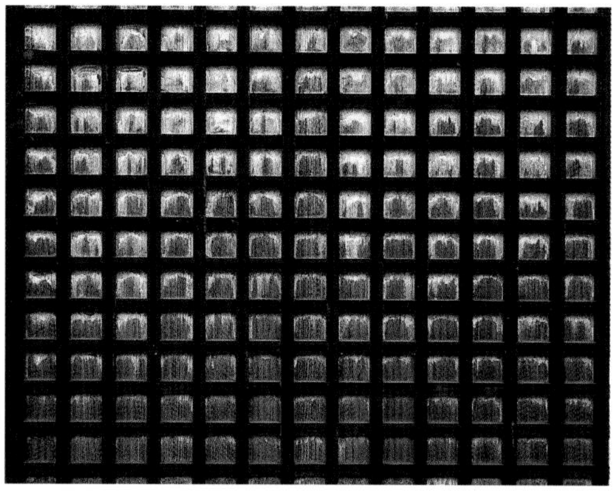
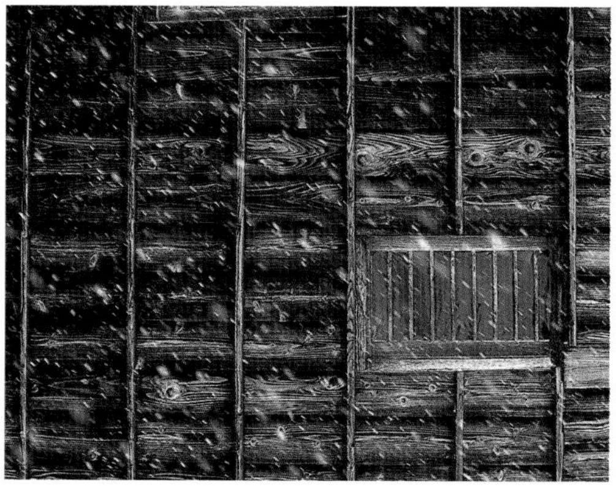
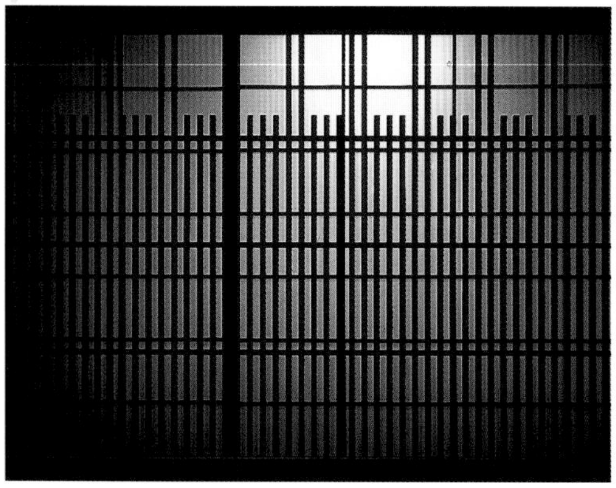
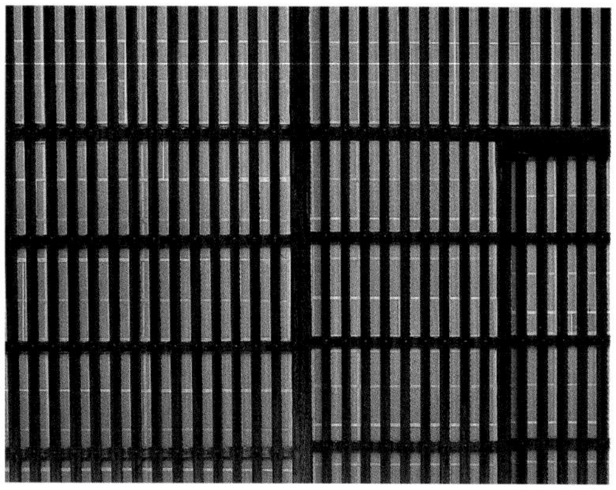
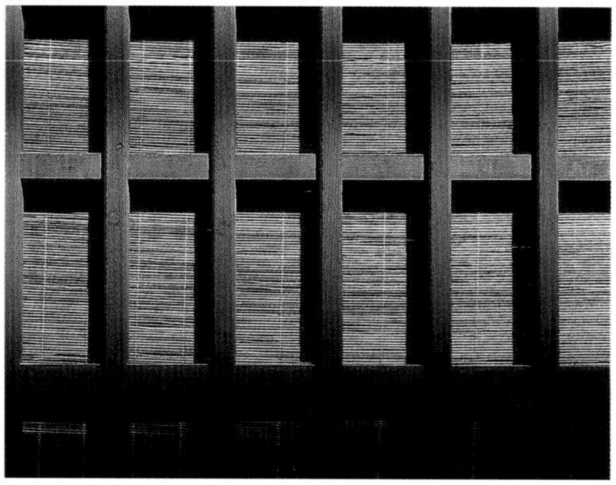

130

Atsumaru

Row upon row of dried fish, vegetables, candies, and rice crackers are signs of plenty and a hint of feasts to come. The endless array of brightly lit paper lanterns and heaps of colorful toys lend a joyous air to a festival on a hot summer night. Collections can excite and charm, but they can also comfort and calm: the procession of stone lanterns leading to a Buddhist sanctuary, the series of *torii* gates on the way to an ancient Shinto shrine are like meditative mandalas. The endless rows of Jizo, patron saint of children who die prematurely, invite us to contemplate the beauty and sadness of life.

Collection

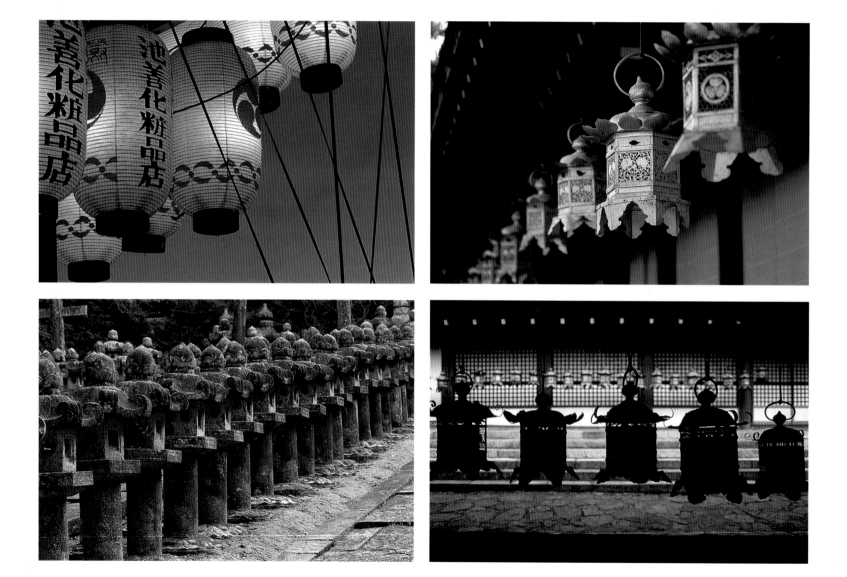

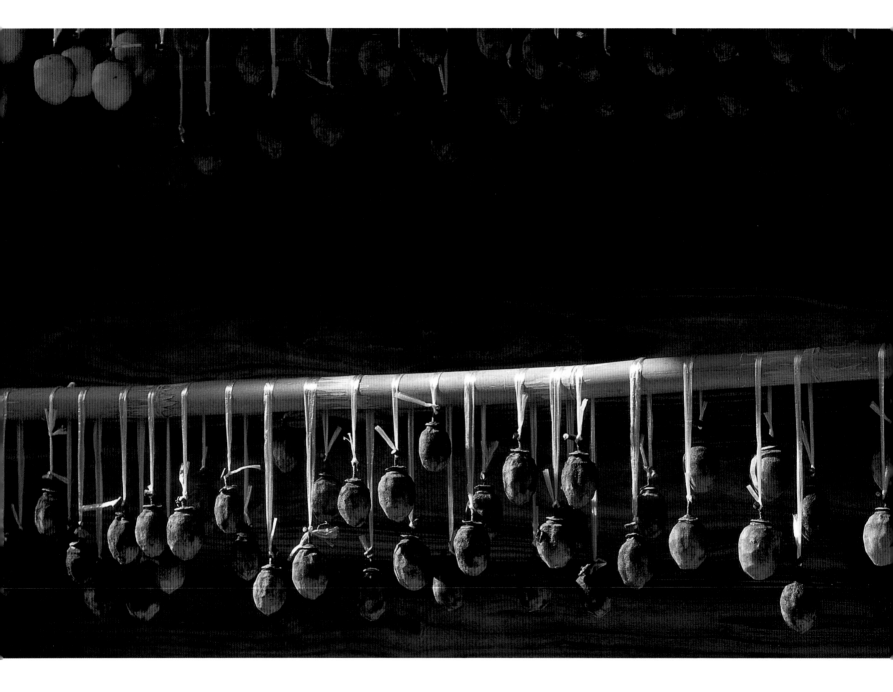

151

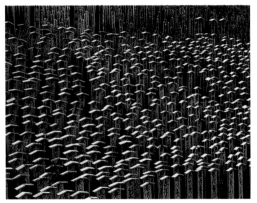

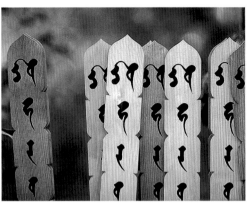

Captions

Foreword and Preface

2–3 Roof tiles embedded in west perimeter wall of Daitokuji temple compound, Kyoto.

4 Brocade Noh costume with design of water, iris, and wisteria, mid-Edo period.

6–7 Roofs of Uiricho fishing village, Noto Peninsula, Ishikawa-ken.

8 Fortune slips tied to lattice of main gate of Kofukuji temple, Nagasaki. Linen *noren* (shop-door curtains) with peach design in Sammachi Suji, Takayama. *Noren* in Sammachi Suji, Takayama. Lattice window of house in Gion, Kyoto. Round *shoji* (sliding paper window) of Kusakabe Mingei-kan, Sammachi Suji, Takayama, ca. 1879. Base of post of Kenchoji temple, Kamakura.

9 *Koinobori* (carp streamers) fluttering in celebration of Boys' Day, May 5.

11 *Mon* on shop-door curtain in Arimatsu, Edo period. Shadow of

fortune slips tied to a spoked circular frame, Iwakisan Shrine, Aomori-ken. Wall of *kura* (storehouse) near Matsuyama. Wall made with roof tiles and clay, samurai quarter, Hagi. Mortise and tenon joint of temple gate, Kenchoji, Kamakura. Garden wall of bamboo and pine boards, Tentoku-in temple, Koyasan, Wakayama.

12 Lantern with cherry blossom design at entrance gate of Tentoku-in temple, Koyasan, Wakayama-ken.

14 *Mon* (family crest) of bamboo on indigo-dyed cotton wedding *furoshiki* (wrapper for presents), 19th c.

15 *Fusuma* (room divider) in historic Nakatani "Lacquer House," Noto, Ishikawa-ken.

17 Oribe-ware *jubako* (tiered food-serving box), with eggplant design, ca. 1820.

Nagare / Flowing

19 Lacquer incense storage box, with wave pattern in silver foil and gold, 18th c.

20 Oil dish for traditional lamp in Oribe green glaze, Seto, Mid-Edo period.

21 Zen garden at Konchi-in temple, Kyoto. River in Miyama-cho, Kyoto-fu.

22 *Shoji* (sliding paper window) and *ramma* (transom) with design of flowing water in a former

druggist's shop in Uchiko, ca. 1915. Detail of window frame with wave pattern and Chinese-style cloud design, from house in Tono, Iwate-ken, mid-18th c. Detail of *ramma* in samurai house, Takezoe-tei, Izumi, Kagoshima-ken, 17th c.

23 Gate to Toshogu Shrine, Nikko.

24 Brocade Noh costume, with wisteria and iris, mid-Edo period. Back of fan used in Japanese dance, Meiji period. Three-season design kimono showing water pattern in gold thread, with *shibori* and embroidered flowers, ca. 1790.

25 Roof tile cap with flowing water pattern, Hakusan Butsudo temple, Ishikawa-ken. Carved bamboo brush stand, Taisho period. Kimono with water design in gold thread, by M. Wada, mid-20th c.

26 Zen garden, Ginkakuji, Kyoto.

27 *Noren* of Mizu Yokan sweet shop. *Fusuma* in Ume-no-ma room at Kongobuji temple, Koyasan, Wakayama-ken. Door of gate at Engakuji temple, Kamakura.

28 Kimono with river and seaside scenes based on *tanka* poem, ca. 1850.

29 Three-season design kimono, ca. 1860.

30 Carp pond, Tokyo. Garden at Shisendo, Kyoto.

31 Mount Fuji-shaped cone at Ginkakuji temple, Kyoto. Garden of Rengejo-in temple, Koyasan,

Wakayama-ken. Garden of Ginkakuji temple, Kyoto. Tokekiko garden of Ryogen-in Zen temple, Daitokuji, Kyoto. Garden in front of Ryogen-in, Daitokuji, Kyoto. Mount Fuji-shaped cone at Ginkakuji temple, Kyoto

32 Detail of Garyu Sanso villa, Ozu, Shikoku. Stone water basin, Daisho-in temple, Hagi, Yamaguchi-ken.

33 Main garden of Shisendo, Kyoto, 17th c.

Maru / Round

35 Tea-room window at Sesshuji temple, Kyoto.

36 Sun motif on man's dancing fan, Taisho period.

37 Tea-room window at Sesshuji temple, Kyoto.

38 Umbrellas drying at maker's shop in Uchiko, Ehime-ken, Shikoku.

39 Umbrella and *shoji* window, Takayama. Underside of umbrella, Kyoto.

40 Back of *happi* (festival coat) with *itsutsu tomoe* design, at Sanja Matsuri festival, Asakusa, Tokyo. Head of a drum with *mitsu tomoe* design at Sanja Matsuri. Lanterns with characters and *mitsu tomoe* designs at Yasaka Shrine, Kyoto.

41 Gong and giant drum with *tomoe* design, Meiji Shrine, Tokyo.

42 Lantern with fan design at temple entrance gate, Koyasan,

Wakayama-ken. Lattice gate at Kofukuji temple, Nagasaki.

43 Storage jar with seashell lid, Kumejima, Okinawa.

44 *Noren* with family crest at shop Funaoka, Gion, Kyoto.

45 Roof tile caps with *mitsu tomoe* design on gate of Yogen-in temple, Kyoto. Roof tile cap on wall with design of three dragon scales, Hokaiji temple, Kamakura.

46 Window in Joboji, an outbuilding of Tendaiji temple, Iwate-ken. Window in Ajiro-no-ma room of Seison-kaku villa, Kenrokuen, Kanazawa.

47 *Noren* of restaurant in Ginza, Tokyo, with design of paulownia leaves and flowers. Crest with hollyhock design at Jochiji temple, Kita Kamakura.

48 Crest with *nibiki* ("two-line") design on lantern at restaurant, Kyoto. Curtain with *tomoe* design at restaurant in Gion, Kyoto.

49 Shop curtains with character for "fortune," Kyoto.

Katadoru / Sign

51 Character for "health" mounted on a scroll.

52 *Noren* of restaurant Kimbei, Ginza, Tokyo.

53 Street sign.

54 *Soba* (buckwheat noodle) shop sign, Kyoto. Signs listing products of a sake maker, Sammachi Suji, Takayama.

55 Signs presenting menu of a restaurant, Sanmachi Suji, Takayama.

56 Poetry mounted as a scroll, late-Edo or Meiji period.

57 Writing on window of *sembei* (rice cracker) maker, Nakamise Dori, Asakusa, Tokyo.

58 Sign of sweet shop Hirosaki, Aomori-ken. Sign at Kofukuji temple, Nagasaki.

59 Window in a door, Tono, Iwate-ken.

60 Bamboo paper weight for calligraphy.

61 Details of various signs: from Kamakura (top right and left); from Choshoji temple, Hirosaki, Aomori-ken; from sweet shop at Takaosan-guchi, Tokyo; on *shoji* door, Furuimachi area, Takayama; and from Higashiyama, Kyoto.

62 Lanterns painted with donor names decorating a float for the Sanja Matsuri festival, Asakusa, Tokyo. Lanterns advertising a restaurant's special tofu dish, Higashiyama, Kyoto. Lantern and neon sign of bar, Ginza, Tokyo. Hanging banners at a small shrine, Oimachi, Tokyo.

63 Banners at the National Theater, Tokyo.

64 *Noren* with pattern of rice measures, symbolizing increasing good fortune, Kyoto.

65 *Noren* with shop trademark, Furuimachi area, Takayama. *Noren* with pattern of rice measures and arrow, Asakusa, Tokyo.

66 Banners at Sugimotodera temple, Kamakura.

67 Base of large hanging lantern at Osu Jinja Shrine, Nagoya. Shop curtain featuring *kanji* for "day," Kyoto.

Sei / Sanctity

69 *Shimenawa*, sacred rope woven of rice straw, on main gate of Iwakisan Shrine, Aomori-ken.

70 Bells hanging at Taketeru Shrine at Iwakiyama, Aomori-ken. Sacred folded paper, *gohei,* at Futarasan Shrine, Nikko.

71 *Shimenawa* and *gohei* at entry to Iwakisan Shrine, Aomori-ken.

72 *Nio,* guardian warrior, with *ofuda,* slips of paper containing prayers for good fortune, at main gate of Tendaiji temple, Iwate-ken.

73 Door of Sensoji temple with *ofuda,* Asakusa, Tokyo. *Shimenawa* and *gohei* at small roadside shrine, Sammachi, Suji, Takayama. *Gohei* at main gate of Hachimangu Shrine, Kamakura.

74 Jizo, stone Buddhist protector figure, Tohoku.

75 Buddha figure carved in living rock at Usuki, Oita-ken, Kyushu. Stone water container with relief of lotus flower and leaves, at graves of the So clan, Tsushima Island, Nagasaki-ken.

76 Sign at Choshoji temple, Hirosaki, Aomori-ken, showing cross-section of grave marker construction. Incense burning at Sensoji temple, Asakusa, Tokyo.

77 Curtain demarcating the sacred zone of Nishi Honganji temple, Kyoto.

78 Detail of lantern with sacred knot symbolizing peace and connectedness, Sorakuen garden, Nakayamate, Kobe. Sand garden of Honen-in temple, Kyoto. Sacred knot at Yasukuni Shrine, Tokyo.

Knotted *shimenawa* at entry gate of Homyoji temple, Miyama-cho, Kyoto. Window at sub-temple of Sensoji, Asakusa, Tokyo. Interior of small shrine with mirror, at Toyokawa Inari Shrine, Aichi-ken.

79 Door hinge at Higashi Honganji temple, Kyoto. Incense burner at the Daibutsu (Great Buddha), Kamakura. Bronze lantern base showing *rei shi* ("never-grow-old plants") design at Daibutsu, Kamakura. Lattice work at small temple, Koyasan, Wakayama-ken. *Shoji* screen and outer door of Choshoji temple, Hirosaki, Aomori-ken. Window at Hokaiji temple, Kamakura.

80 Buddha figure, and stone incised with Buddha image, Engakuji temple, Kita Kamakura. Rows of Buddhas at Sanjusangendo temple, Kyoto.

81 *Rakan,* Buddhist saints, in mountain cave at Rakanji temple, Oita-ken, Kyushu.

82 Daikoku, often depicted standing on rice bales, over door of public bath, Kita Senju, Tokyo. Small guardian *nio* to protect from fire, over a house entrance, Gion, Kyoto. Small *nio* over restaurant entrance, Gion, Kyoto. Demon holding up the roof beam of the gate at Henjoko-in temple, Koyasan, Wakayama-ken. Stone figure at Fukiji temple, Oita-ken, Kyushu. Stone Jizo, protector of children and travelers, at side of country road, Oita-ken, Kyushu.

83 Guardian warrior at Sugimotodera temple, Kamakura.

84 Painting of dragon on *fusuma* room divider, Ryogen-in temple, Daitokuji, Kyoto, Edo period.

85 Scroll with character *ryu* for "dragon," Edo period.

86 Detail of scroll-mounted fabric with design of dragon in gold thread, Edo period.

87 *Amaryu*, "rain dragons," on blue Oribe-ware dishes for oil lamps, 18th c.

88 Woven phoenix design with lightning and clouds on table cover, Edo period.

89 View through entrance gate to Joyoden Hall at Eiheiji temple, Echizen, Fukui-ken, with phoenix and other fanciful figures carved in the wooden *ramma*.

90 Detail of child's kimono with phoenix and peony design, early 20th c.

91 Phoenix on *noren* of shop in Sammachi Suji, Takayama. Phoenix and pauwlonia leaves on *tsutsugaki* (paste-resist-dyed cotton cloth), Meiji period. Phoenix carved in wood and lacquered, in fence of Fukutoku Inari Shrine, Mount Takao, Tokyo. Phoenix on metal lock plate of *tansu* (traditional chest), from Miyagi-ken, early Meiji period.

92 *Shishi*, "lion dogs," on base of a large bronze lotus at the Daibutsu, Kamakura. *Shishi* under the roof peak of gate at Henjoko-in temple, Koyasan, Wakayama-ken. *Shishi* carved in wooden outer door of Fugenjin temple, Koyasan, Wakayama-ken. Pair of *shishi* in lacquered wood, outer wall of Yomeimon Gate, Toshogu Shrine, Nikko.

93 Ceramic *shishi*, likely from Okinawa, over entry to restaurant, Gion, Kyoto.

Sei / Nature

95 Cranes and willow on gold-leaf *fusuma* in Willow Room, Kongobuji temple, Koyasan, Wakayama-ken.

96 Door curtain of traditional Japanese sweet shop, Kyoto. Crane and character for "forever" in roof tile cap, Kameoka, Kyoto-fu. *Noren* of teahouse with three interlocking cranes, Higashiyama, Kyoto. *Noren* of tea shop with two cranes and *noshi*, a felicitous decoration, Kamakura.

97 Crane on Seto-ware dish, late-Edo period.

98 Design of cranes on Kyogen costume for a child, mid-Meiji period.

99 Flying crane on gold leaf *fusuma*, Rengejoin temple, Koyasan, Wakayama-ken.

100 Tiger design on ikat bedding cover, cotton, 19th c.

101 Tiger painting on scroll, Edo period.

102 Cotton *furoshiki* with design of mandarin ducks, plum, and bamboo, with chrysanthemum design crest, from Fukuoka-ken, 19th c.

103 Painted *ema* (votive plaque) of horse at shrine near Hirosaki, Aomori-ken. Straw effigy of horse at small shrine by the Japan Sea, Takagurose, Yamaguchi-ken.

104 Crows on painted wall panel, Iwakisan Shrine, Aomori-ken. Fish on painted wall panel, Iwakisan Shrine, Aomori-ken.

105 Heron in winter scene painted on wooden *fusuma*, Willow Room, Kongobuji temple, Koyasan, Wakayma-ken.

106 Sculpted stone water basin at house entrance, eastern geisha district, Kanazawa. Koi in pool at Glover Garden, Nagasaki.

107 Tails and streamers of *koinobori*, carp streamers to celebrate Boys' Day.

108 Kimono, ca. 1840. Box with design of autumn plants in gold and red lacquer.

109 Seto-ware oil dish, 19th c.

110 Cotton ikat bedding cover of *shochikubai* (pine, plum, and bamboo) design, late-Edo or early Meiji period. Cotton *tsutsugaki* bedding cover with dyed *shochikubai* design from Fukuoka-ken, Kyushu, mid-Meiji period.

111 Large Imari plate with *shochikubai* design, late 18th c.

112 Two sheets of chrysanthemum and dragonfly designs for stenciling ceramics, lacquer on leather. Top of lacquer box with gold design of gourd vines, late-Edo period.

113 Fan with seasonal scenes of spring and autumn, Meiji period.

114 Kimono sash with design of cherry blossoms and maple leaf, Taisho or early Showa period. View of *shoji* through *ramma* with design of gourds on the vine, Garyu Sanso Villa, Ozu, Ehime-ken. Dry sweets in autumn motifs, Kyoto.

115 Young woman's kimono showing summer motifs of rice and water, ca. 1830.

116 Temple door with *mon* in design of *tachibana*, a wild orange, Wajima, Noto, Ishikawa-ken.

117 Brocade kimono sash with design of waves, pine, plum, cranes, and bamboo, Meiji period. Ikat kimono with design of violets, early 20th c. *Noren* with design of trees, Kyoto. Brocade sash with design of pine and tortoise, Meiji period. Ikat summer kimono with design of water, Taisho period. Brocade sash with design of tea leaves, late-Edo or early Meiji period. Ikat summer kimono with design of maple leaves, Taisho or early Showa period. Silk ikat kimono with Okinawan motif of birds and flowers, early 20th c. Ikat summer kimono with design of water and snails.

Kata / Pattern

119 Lattice window of house, Takayama.

120 Street side of garden wall, Takayama.

121 *Shoji* with shadows of bamboo lattice, in tea ceremony room of Zuiho-in Zen temple, Daitokuji, Kyoto.

122 Bamboo fence of house in Gion, Kyoto.

123 Exterior of Ichirikijaya teahouse in Gion, Kyoto. Exterior of restaurant in Gion, Kyoto. Front of house in Noto, Ishikawa-ken. Exterior of restaurant, Kyoto.

124 Lattice over *shoji* of house, Sammachi Suji, Takayama.

125 Lattice over *shoji* of house, Sammachi Suji, Takayama.

126 Fence protecting *nio*, guardian figure, in inner gate of Hachimangu Shrine, Kamakura.

127 Bamboo screen at Shinto shrine, Nara.

128 Details of various lattice window and door grills, at: Sammachi Suji, Takayama; samurai district, Hagi, Yamaguchi-ken; Furuimachi area, Takayama; Sammachi Suji, Takayama; Sammachi Suji, Takayama; entrance to Ono temple, Fukui-ken; Sensoji temple, Asakusa, Tokyo; Gangoji temple, Nara; farm outbuilding near Nojiriko lake, Nagano-ken; house near Nanzenji temple, Kyoto; Narai, Nakasendo; Sammachi Suji, Takayama.

129 Various bamboo screens, fences, and shades, at: Tsumago, Nakasendo; Sammachi Suji, Takayama; temple, Kyoto; Kamakura; temple garden, Koyasan, Wakayama-ken; Katsura Villa, Kyoto; teahouse, Kyoto; teahouse, Higashiyama, Kyoto; Rengejoin temple, Koyasan, Wakayama-ken; old house, Gion, Kyoto; garden, Muromachi area, Kyoto; Sammachi Suji, Takayama.

130 Temple gate, Nagasaki. Wall of fishing shed near Mikkabi, Hamanako lake, Shizuoka-ken. Gate of house, Kita Village, Miyama-cho, Kyoto. Shop wall, Higashiyama, Kyoto.

131 Wall and door of *kura,* Kiso Fukushima, Nagano-ken.

132 Wall of building, Ukawa town, Noto, Ishikawa-ken.

133 Side of *jubako* (tiered food-serving box), Oribe ware, ca. 1820.

134 Walls of samurai quarter, Hagi, Yamaguchi-ken. Stone garden and typhoon wall, Shitaru,

Tsushima Island, Nagasaki-ken. Retaining wall, Kenchoji temple, Kamakura. Out-side yard wall, Nakatani "Lacquer House," Noto, Ishikawa-ken.

135 Wall and roofline of *kura,* Miyama-cho, Kyoto-fu. Window of *kura,* Miyama-cho, Kyoto-fu. Portholes for defense, Himeji-jo castle, Himeji. Wall and window of *kura* near Nojiriko lake, Nagano-ken.

136 Cotton ikat bedding cover, Meiji period.

137 Street wall of temple, Koyasan, Wakayama-ken. Wall of *kura,* near Iida, Nagano-ken.

138 Tiled roofs, Noto, Ishikawa-ken. Entry path to traditional restaurant, Takayama.

139 Tie-dyed summer kimono, Aichi-ken, Taisho or early Showa period.

Atsumaru / Collection

141 Lanterns on float, Gion Matsuri festival, Kyoto.

142 Various lantens, in paper, metal, and stone, at: Yasaka Shrine, Kyoto; Kamigamo Shrine, Kyoto; Daisho-in temple, Hagi, Yamaguchi-ken; Kasuga Wakamiya Shrine, Nara.

143 Lanterns at Miedo temple, Koyasan, Wakayama-ken.

144 Paper and bamboo ceremonial umbrellas, Gion Matsuri, Kyoto. Paper umbrellas at Yakunou-in temple, Mount Takao, Tokyo.

145 Traditional soda bottles at festival, Tokyo.

146 Persimmons drying, Kagoshima-ken.

147 Fish grilling on sticks at festival, Asakusa, Tokyo. Bundled greens on roadside, Mount Ontakesan. *Hokigusa,* brush used to make brooms, drying, Aomori-ken. Onions hanging to dry, Tsushima Island, Nagasaki-ken.

148 Donor's plaques at Shorenji temple, Takayama. Straw mats and nets drying outside a restaurant, Kyoto.

149 Wishes written on *ema* at Iwakisan Shrine, Aomori-ken.

150 Multitude of stone Jizo, protector of children who died prematurely, and grave markers, Nembutsudera, Kyoto.

151 *Hamaya,* "devil-shooting arrow," offered to shrine visitors at New Year's for good fortune in the coming year, Asakusa, Tokyo. Figures of Daruma, a bringer good fortune, for sale at Asakusa, Tokyo.

152 Fans for sale on Nakamise Dori, street leading to Sensoji temple, Asakusa, Tokyo.

153 Pile of Daruma figures returned to shrine at end of year, Kanazawa.

154 Wooden votive slats, Haguro-yama. Folded paper cranes, Fushimi Inari Shrine, Kyoto. Dried fish at outdoor market. Marinated fish drying in Izuhara, Tsushima Island, Nagasaki-ken. *Ema* at Hachimangu Shrine, Kamakura. Slats bearing posthumous Buddhist names at Hokaiji

temple, Kamakura. Water toys on display in Ginza, Tokyo. *Torii* gates at Shorenji temple, Takayama. Prayer slips tied to fence at Hachimangu Shrine, Kamakura. *Sembei* (rice crackers) at shop in Takaosan-guchi, Tokyo. Children's masks for sale at festival, Kamakura. *Ema* at Kanazawa Shrine, Kenrokuen, Kanazawa

155 Close-up of *mikoshi* (portable shrine) at Sanja Matsuri festival, Tokyo.

The "weathermark" identifies this book as a production of Weatherhill, Inc., publishers of fine books on Asia and the Pacific. Editorial supervision: Ray Furse. Book and cover design: Liz Trovato and Kenneth Straiton. Production supervision: Bill Rose. Printing and binding: O. G. Printing Productions, Limited. The typefaces used are Bembo and Trajan.